Hubble's Pasture
&
The Truth About Cows

Written and illustrated by
Peter K.K. Williams

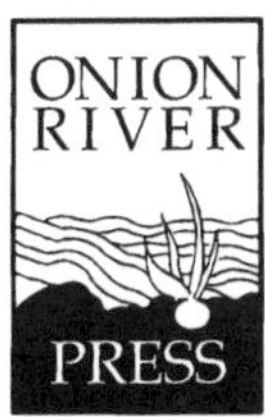

Burlington, Vermont

Interior design and pre-press:
www.tilmanreitzledesign.com

Onion River Press
191 Bank Street
Burlington, Vermont 05401

ISBN: 978-1-957184-15-9
Library of Congress Control Number: 2022914260

September

THE EARLY DAYS OF SEPTEMBER exhibit little change from the giddy whirl of high summer. Sunshine is abundant, the weather mild and vegetation has reached its verdant peak. White, disk-shaped blossoms of Queen Anne's lace tilt this way and that like so many diminutive spiral galaxies adrift in a firmament of green. Hundreds of acres of ripe corn stand seven feet tall, rustling a papery rasp with every breath of wind. The leaves in the vast majority of the forest's deciduous trees are still green, although an isolated maple is already ablaze in red. Milkweed seedpods continue to swell. Soon they will split open and liberate an airborne armada of fluff-borne seeds. Some will alight nearby, others will waft for miles, but all face the challenge of finding a hospitable spot to germinate.

The cows know that September offers the best conditions for viewing the celestial firmament. Nights are often cool and clear and provide the steady air essential for what astronomers call "good seeing." The full harvest moon rises as round and orange as a freshly baked pumpkin pie, but will pale and lose all color as it continues to rise. On cloudless, moonless nights the herd stays up late to observe the Milky Way's vast sneeze of starlight. Spanning the entire zenith, a celestial sight denied to all obliged to live surrounded by light pollution. Our galaxy's gauzy swath, as viewed from our position in the cosmic hinterland known as the outer rim of the Orion Arm, would appear larger and brighter were it not for the great rift, a veil of obscuring gas and dust.

The constellation Cygnus—the swan—looms overhead with wings out-stretched, beak ever-pointed towards the central hub of our own galactic pinwheel. The stars that form the constellation Saggitarious create an asterism, an outline of a teapot whose spout appears to emit a steamy vapor of starlight.

Although their numbers have been depleted in recent years, Monarch but-terflies know that September is a transitional month. Every year these intrepid aeronauts undertake a heroic migratory flight whose ultimate goal is Mexico. They depart on a glorious high-pressure September afternoon beneath a sun-drenched cerulean sky, adhering to a flight-path unrecognized by even the most astute air-traffic controller. Completion of this epic round-trip journey will require the combined efforts of several generations of Monarchs. Inevitably, somewhere along the way a Monarch will alight on the moist pink nose of a cow.

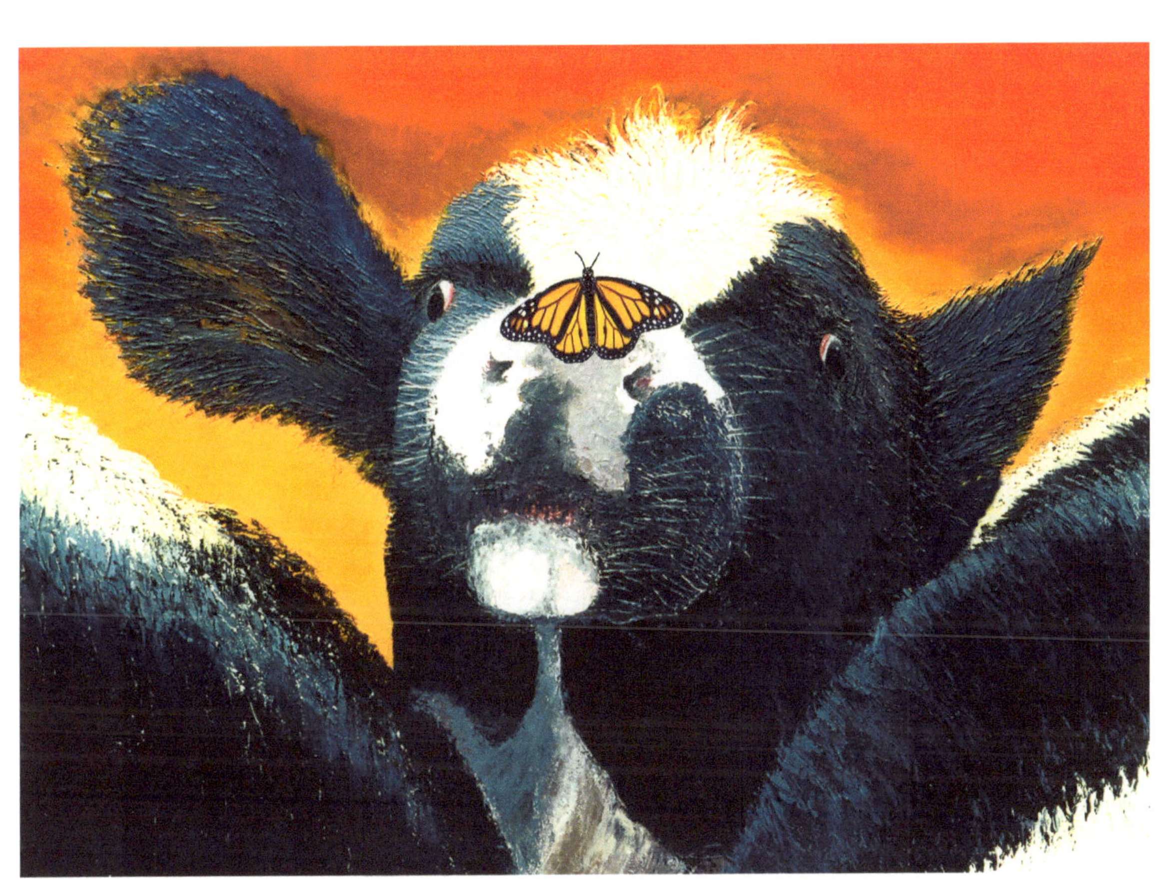

October

LEAVES ONCE GREEN AND GLOSSY now exhibit variations of red, yellow, orange and russet, along with damage inflicted by countless insect mandibles. Mother Nature abandons her reliance on green as the more colorful cells within each leaf overwhelm summer's dominant hue. Initially, a solitary leaf detaches and glides gracefully to the ground. Minutes later another lets go. The rate gradually increases until the ground is carpeted with leaves as crisp as potato chips, to eventually create a mirror between the colorful carpet under hoof and the remaining leaves in the canopy overhead.

By mid-month a light frost touches the colder hollows. Soon, the first hard frost of the season wilts every plant, grounds the bumblebees and sends the chipmonks dashing for their mufflers. These attractively striped rodents emit a sharp chirp at the first sign of danger, real or imagined, but however cute they may be, a chipmunk is nothing more than a rat wearing an L.L. Bean sports coat. As the month progresses, chilly wind-driven rain strips the branches. Soggy fallen leaves turn brown and emit the unmistakable odor of autumnal decay, as evocative as the aroma of newly mown grass. Most trees stand naked by the time the month has ended.

Stick season has begun. The color green has vanished except for grass, ferns, moss, conifers and Vermont license plates. The rising sun's waning strength takes longer to dispel the morning chill. Tepid sunlight melts the frost-rimed grass to reveal a sparkling green swathe, while the shaded penumbra beneath spruces

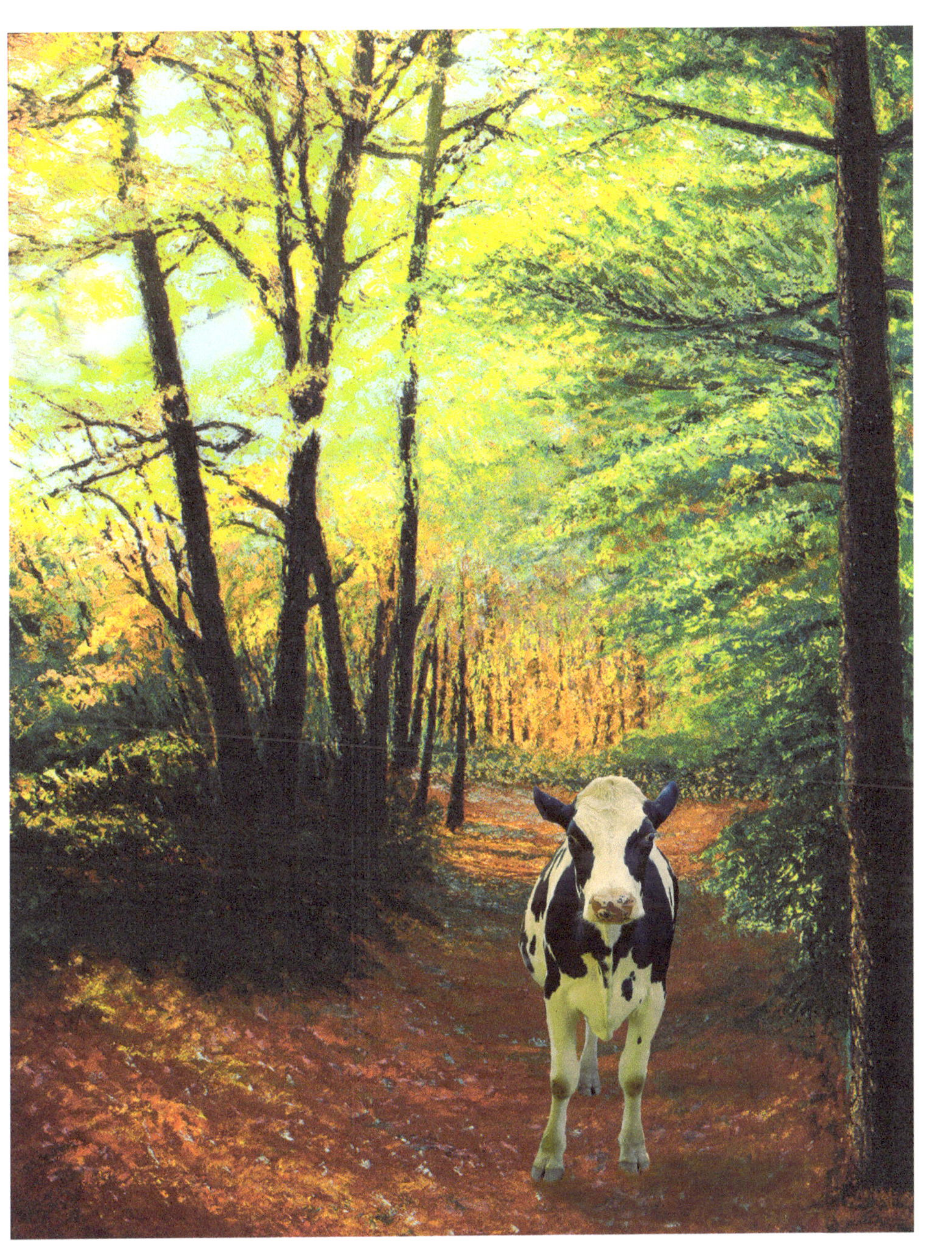

remains white with frost. The return of midday warmth inspires yet another bravura performance by the renowned Hillpharmonic. Resplendent in a green tuxedo, a praying mantis conducts the Autumn Concerto. Honeybees thrum in the bass section, while male crickets murmur sweet nothings into the tympanic mebrane of their beloved; a process known as stridulation. The robust keening dwindles as falling temperatures induce a somber diminuendo. The renewed warmth of Indian summer provides a brief respite and inspires an encore.

The Pleiades rise in the eastern sky as evening accedes to night. Anchored eternally to the ground and unaware of the literary tradition engendered by the cow that jumped over the moon, the herd hears raucous squawking from high above. A southbound flock of geese flies overhead in V formation, honking exuberantly. The tip of the V is the most prestigious position, as any goose can attest, but if a goose wishes to acquire status, it must wait until the point-goose tires and relinquishes its place.

The aerodynamics encountered at the tip of the V are complex and involve windspeed, slipstreaming, celestial navigation and only a goose knows what. The cows lift their heads and stare in mute wonder as the flock recedes into the distance. The sound of honking dwindles until only silence remains, at which point the cows heave a collective sigh and trudge wearily from meadow to barn, leaving deep hoof imprints in the mud.

November

NOVEMBER is a tedious month for herd and herdsmen alike. The sky is reduced to a low opaque ceiling that smothers the peaks of the Green Mountains as if by some monstrous grey broody hen. Ghostly wraiths of vapor glide across their flanks. The cows have all but forgotten what a blue-sky looks like. Only a faint smudge behind the clouds suggests the continued existence of the sun. Chilly winds have stripped away the last of the dead leaves that stubbornly clung to elm branches. Milkweed pods have all burst, their seeds scattered to the four winds. On such a solumn morning the cows venure outdoors, aware that the weather is only going to get a lot worse before it gets any better.

The hummingbirds that zoomed from blossom to blossom all summer have returned to the rainforests of Costa Rica. Robins migrated to warmer climes, although not as far south. The seagulls that loiter all summer near Lake Champlain still haunt the parking lot of hamburger emporiums; they land on the hood of cars, beady yellow eyes fixed on the ketchup-smeared fries being consumed within. Snowbirds migrate to Florida via interstate highway but the chickadees stay, puffing up their feathers to cheerfully endure winter's wrath. Barred owls waft silently through the air before perching on tree limbs, ever alert for the telltale rustle of a careless mouse.

Deer hunting season in Vermont begins in mid-November. For the next two weeks every cow, horse and dog faces the prospect of being shot. The deer are aware of their peril and make themselves scarce. Hunters clad in orange

Day-Glo roam the hills; most are careful but there are always one or two trigger-happy galoots determined to shoot first and ask questions later. This is why dairymen have been known to paint "cow" in large red letters on the broad flanks of their charges.

The cows know that November is the worst month of the year for stargazing, rivaled only by April for long stretches of cloudiness. Yet in spite of this, the herd looks forward to the Leonid meteor shower, celestial fireworks that recur every year on November 19th. Viewing conditions are seldom favorable, but every now and then the clouds part long enough to afford a glimpse of the cosmic spitballs that zip across the predawn sky. Each Leonid is a shard cast off by a comet that hurtled by in the past. Every year the Earth passes through this residual debris as it orbits the glowing golf ball that is our sun. When a fragment strikes the atmosphere at three times the speed of sound the resulting friction etches an incandescent streak against a sable background. All but the largest are incinerated and occasionally one hits the ground.

Occasionally a larger meteor known as a bolide produces a brilliant green flash; on a winter's night the glare illuminates the snow-covered ground for a split second. In November the temperature often dips below freezing. The higher peaks become draped in white, although the valleys have yet to don ermine cloaks. The cold light of dawn reveals ground-hugging mist as fields relinquish the last vestiges of warmth, a diaphonous exhalation composed of fading summer memories. Only then do the cows recall the previous year's strident lesson… In Vermont, winter is never very far away.

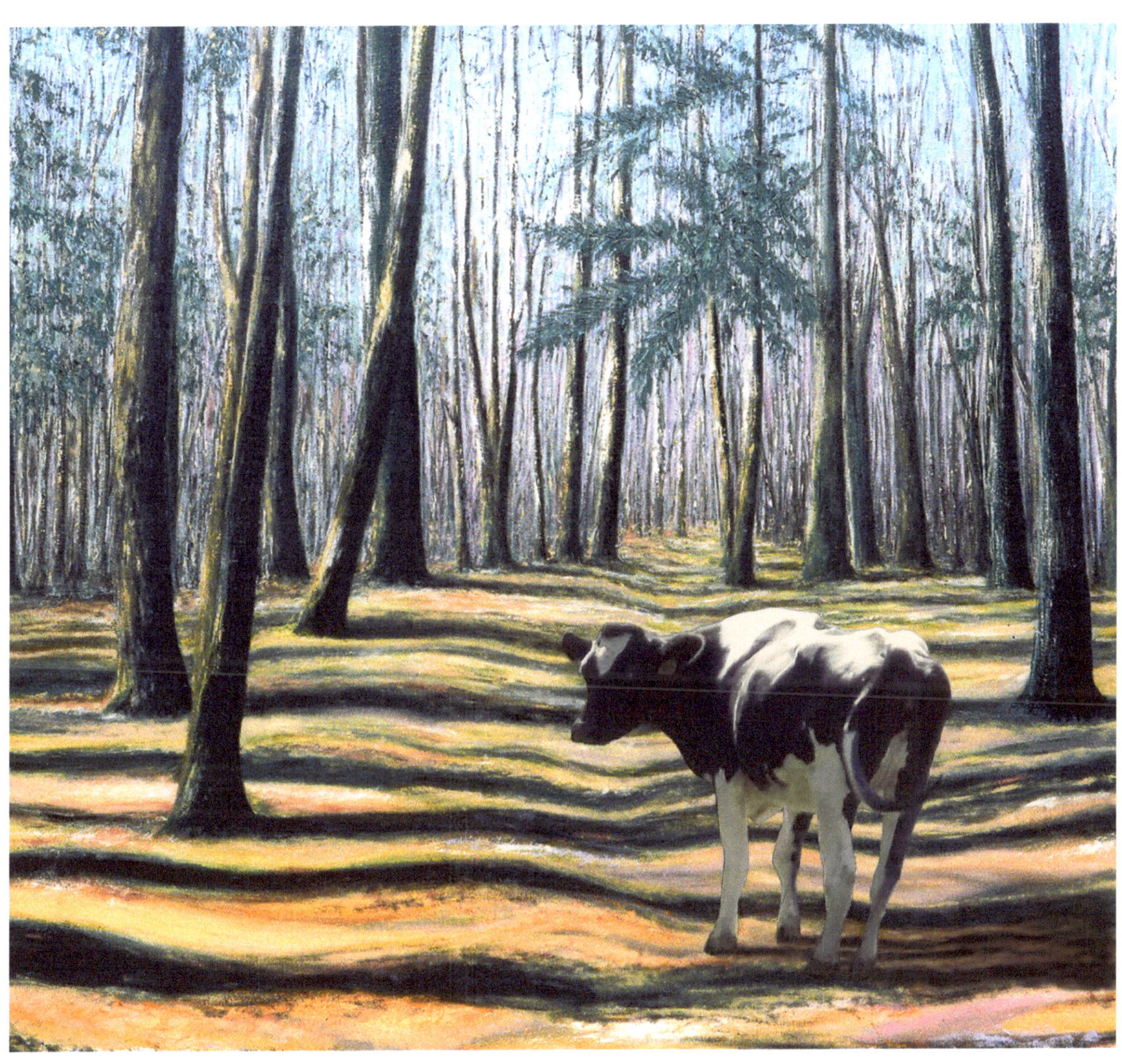

December

DAWN REVEALS A LATTICE of tree limbs obscured by fog. All color has leached from the land. Skeletal trees surround fields fallow and forlorn. What began high above as rain encountered colder air closer to the ground and now every twiglet is glazed with ice. Tree limbs unable to bear the weight break and fall onto power lines, disrupting the flow of electricity and forcing the dairymen to fire up a generator to avoid having to squeeze udders the old fashioned way, by hand.

The herd now spends most of the day in the barn, a drafty unheated structure feebly lit by dangling 40-watt bulbs. With the exception of Edison's glass orbs, little within the barn distinguishes the current century from any that preceeded. Sleet clinks against the metal roof, usurping the patter of late autumn rain. The barn's floor is a glutinous porridge composed of sawdust, mud and straw. A full-grown cow can weigh up to 1,400 pounds. Dairymen know that cows that stand on a soft surface will live longer than those that trod upon concrete.

For elderly dairymen, the time has come to retire and sell the farm—lock, stock and barrel—before moving to Florida. The more adventurous will settle in Key West, where they'll don sunglasses, drink orange juice laced with rum, read Hemingway and begin to thaw the solid blue ice at the core of all crotchety old Vermonters. The less adventurous will settle inland surrounded by shopping malls that stretch as far as the eye can see. The cows, on the other hoof, have no such options; for the herd, moving to Florida is about as likely as moving to Jupiter.

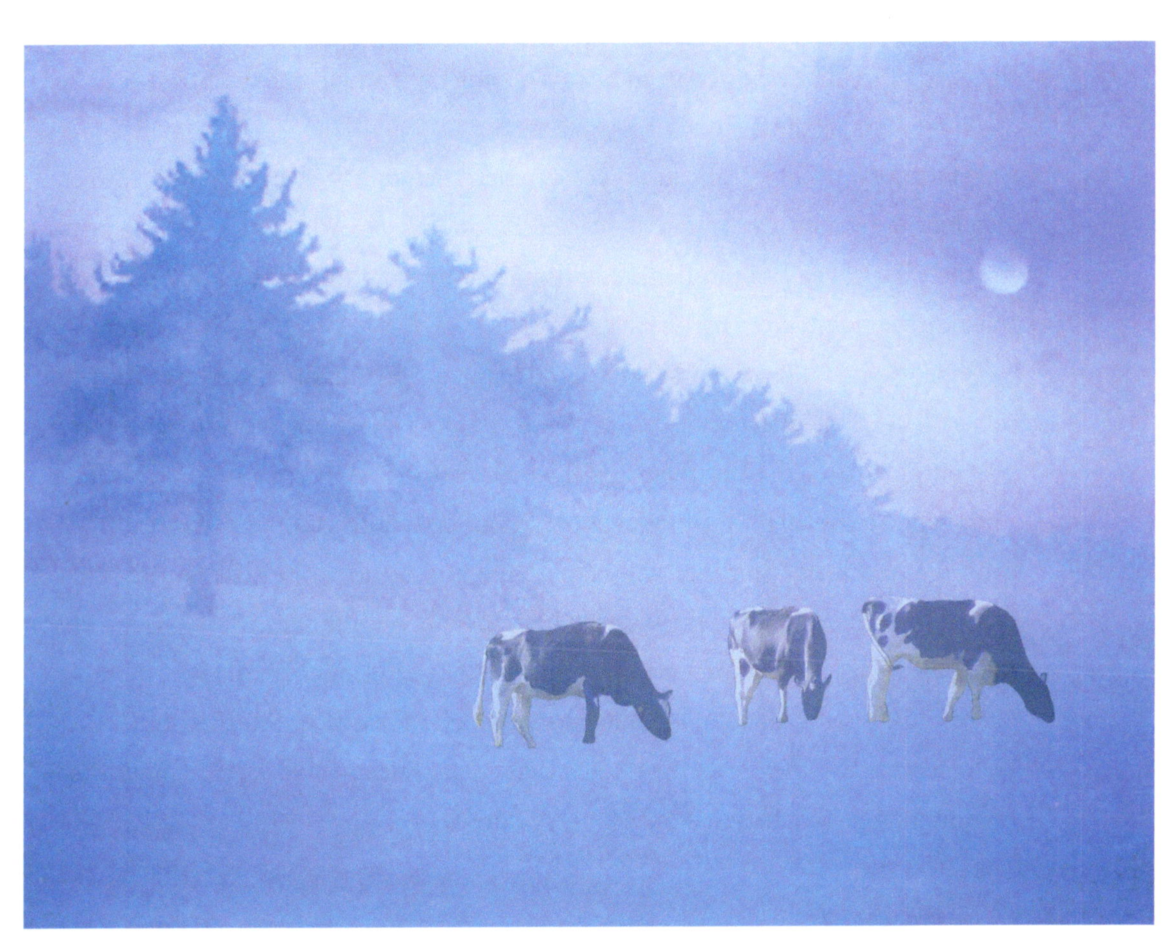

The older and wiser cows are aware of an ineluctable truth . . . climate equals temperament. It's no accident the running of the bulls takes place on the hot, arid streets of Pamplona, an outbreak of lunacy undreamed of in Brattleboro, where the only lapse in bovine decorum occurs during the annual sashay known as "The Strolling of the Heifers."

Each year on a pleasant summer day a herd saunters the length of Main Street, cheered on by a crowd of equally casual onlookers. No young daredevils sprint for their lives ahead of rampaging bulls and not every runner is sufficiently fleet to elude the pointed horns.

On the 21st, the winter solstice heralds the longest night of the year. The sun sets at 4:13 in the afternoon, the last light of a very short day quickly fades from pale purple to grey to black. Darkness prevails by five and by six it might as well be midnight. An overnight dusting of snow amounts to little more than dandruff, but soon the first major snowfall will blanket the ground in white. The constellation Cygnus dips ever closer to the western horizon at about the same time Orion rises in the east. The temperature is a mite nippy for stargazing, but nevertheless, the cows observe the bright, diamond-points that comprise the sword attached to Orion's belt, unaware that the one in the middle is not a star but a nebula, an enormous shell of luminous gas where new stars are being born.

January

A NEW YEAR has begun, along with old man winter's annual test of endurance, their arrival proclaimed by bone-chilling gusts that wrenched and then scattered the pages of a calendar that hung just inside the barn. Older dairymen recall a time in January when the mercury in thermometers plunged to ten degrees below zero and stayed there for a week. Today, a stoked woodstove still prevents cryogenic preservation. Larger stoves are named "Invincible" and "Intrepid," while the smaller are merely "Impertinent."

The herd, however, has never experienced so much as a minute of wood-fired comfort. No double-glazed windows bar the wind's entry, no pink insulation pads the walls and no solar panels transmit warmth to pipes embedded beneath the floor. The only creature comforts available to the cows are their fellow creatures. An adult cow radiates a surprising amount of heat. And so they huddle like male penguins enduring Antarctic privation (while the females are off cavorting in warmer waters, gorging on krill and having a good time). The cows console one another with the fact that they are not obliged to endure hundred mile an hour gales with a temperature of seventy degrees below zero, let alone ridiculously futile attempts to incubate an egg on the top of their toes—or a block of ice, in lieu of an egg.

January is the ideal month for the cows to indulge in morbid introspection, as there is little else to do. Nothing moves outside the barn except falling snow, windwhipped tree limbs and clouds. When the temporary reprieve known as the January thaw sends the temperature soaring into the thirties, the herd becomes giddy with relief.

Similarly inspired, the dairymen shed greasy parkas, manure-besmirched overalls and boots and caper about in thermal underwear with wry smiles on their grizzled faces. The first hint of an approaching blizzard often appears as a ring of ice crystals encircling the sun. The clear blue sky slowly congeals into a milky opacity that blots out our nearest star. Having accreted around a speck of dust or a microbe, a haze of very small but very determined snowflakes signals the onset. Snowflakes begin to descend in much the same shape but differing atmospheric conditions whittle each flake into any of thirty-five different shapes. The winds howl. Blowing snow produces a white-out and only the abominable snowman dares ventures outside, as do dairymen forced to dig a tunnel from house to barn.

Cows and humans share a simple pleasure unknown to all that have never experienced the profound isolation imposed by a Vermont blizzard. Safe and warm within the farmhouse, their chores done, dairymen wait out the storm secure in the knowledge that the refrigerator is well-stocked and an ample supply of split dry firewood lies stacked nearby. There is nowhere to go, even if they could get there. Safe and not so warm in the barn, the cows listen to the wind as it shrieks through the rafters and rattles the walls.

Although the rate of snowfall is measured in inches per hour, the herd nervously awaits the arrival of one gargantuan, six-sided flake that measures three feet thick and a hundred miles wide. They're convinced it's only a matter of time before such a behemoth plummets from on high, hits the ground and delivers a shuddering knockout punch.

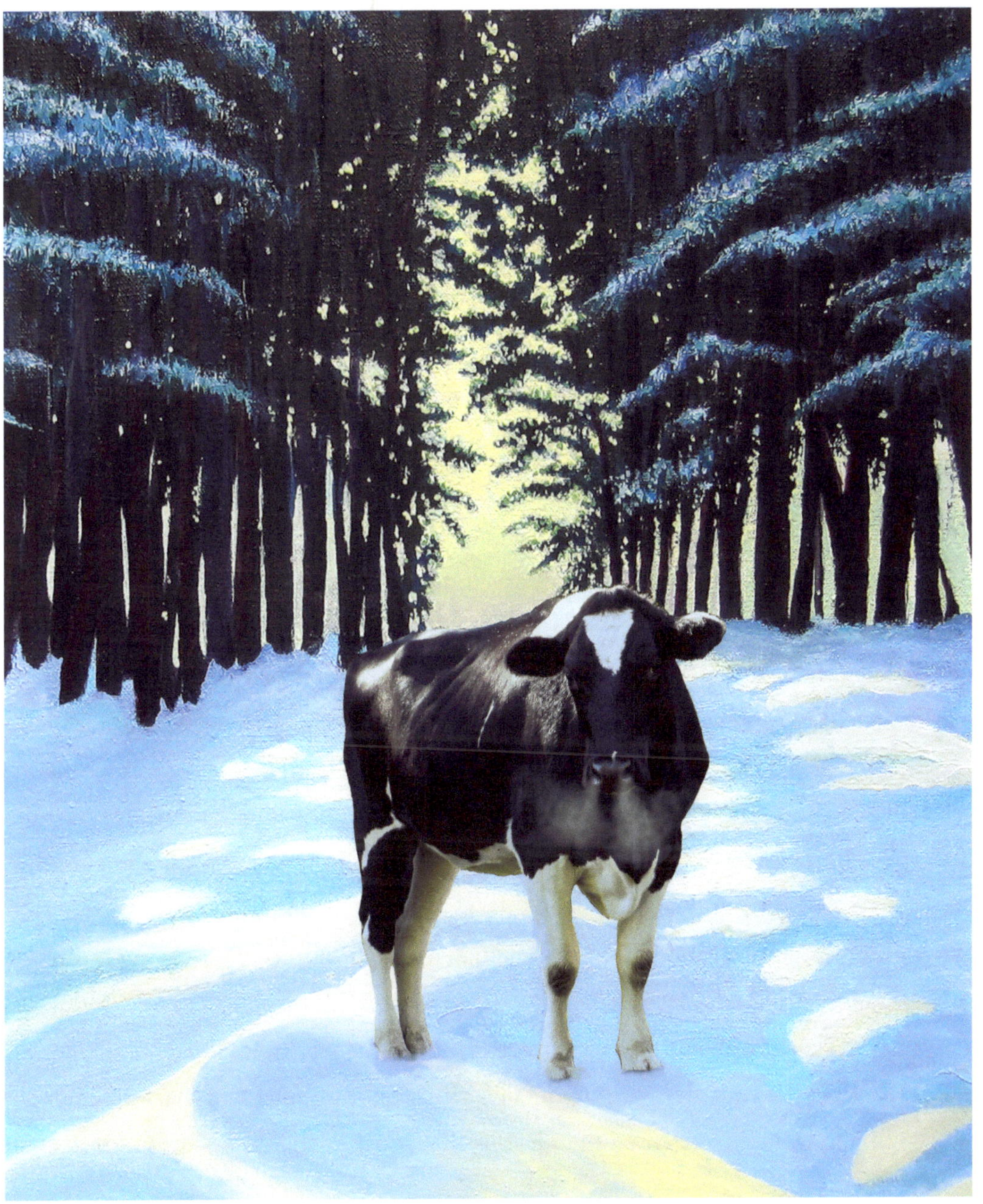

February

February is the shortest month of the year but the cows all agree it seems to last the longest. When not hidden by clouds, the sun hangs low in the sky. Daylight is all too brief. Spring may only be weeks away but it seems more distant, in spite of a minute being added to the length of each day. Even so, when a cow stands in a sunny, windsheltered nook at midday, the sun's warmth is palpable, albeit brief. The sun now sets around five, twilight is fleeting and every time a cow turns around it's dark again.

Yet in spite of the month's dreary regimen, the daily ritual of milking and feeding must be assiduously observed, to say nothing of mucking out the stalls. Prior to tackling these chores, the dairymen consume "lumberjack specials"—a lofty stack of flapjacks smothered in maple syrup, topped with a cackle-berry or two (eggs) and washed down with as many cups of coffee as needed to face the day.

Breakfast for the herd consists of Barn-Mix Granola; a scrumptious blend of oats, corn, hay, sugar and a dash of tripotassium phosphate to ensure freshness. Each cow lowers its shaggy head into the trough—tongue swabbing, jaws gnashing, ears twitching and tail thwacking. An air of bovine contentment fills the barn. The muted sound of munching is punctuated by the sound of splashing as one cow after another empties its bladder with an impressive display of savoir-faire.

Udders bulging, the cows amble to the milking parlor for the first milking of the day. On the way they tread upon an earthen floor imbued with bacteria nourished by the wastes excreted by the pigeons that roost in the rafters, trespassers reviled

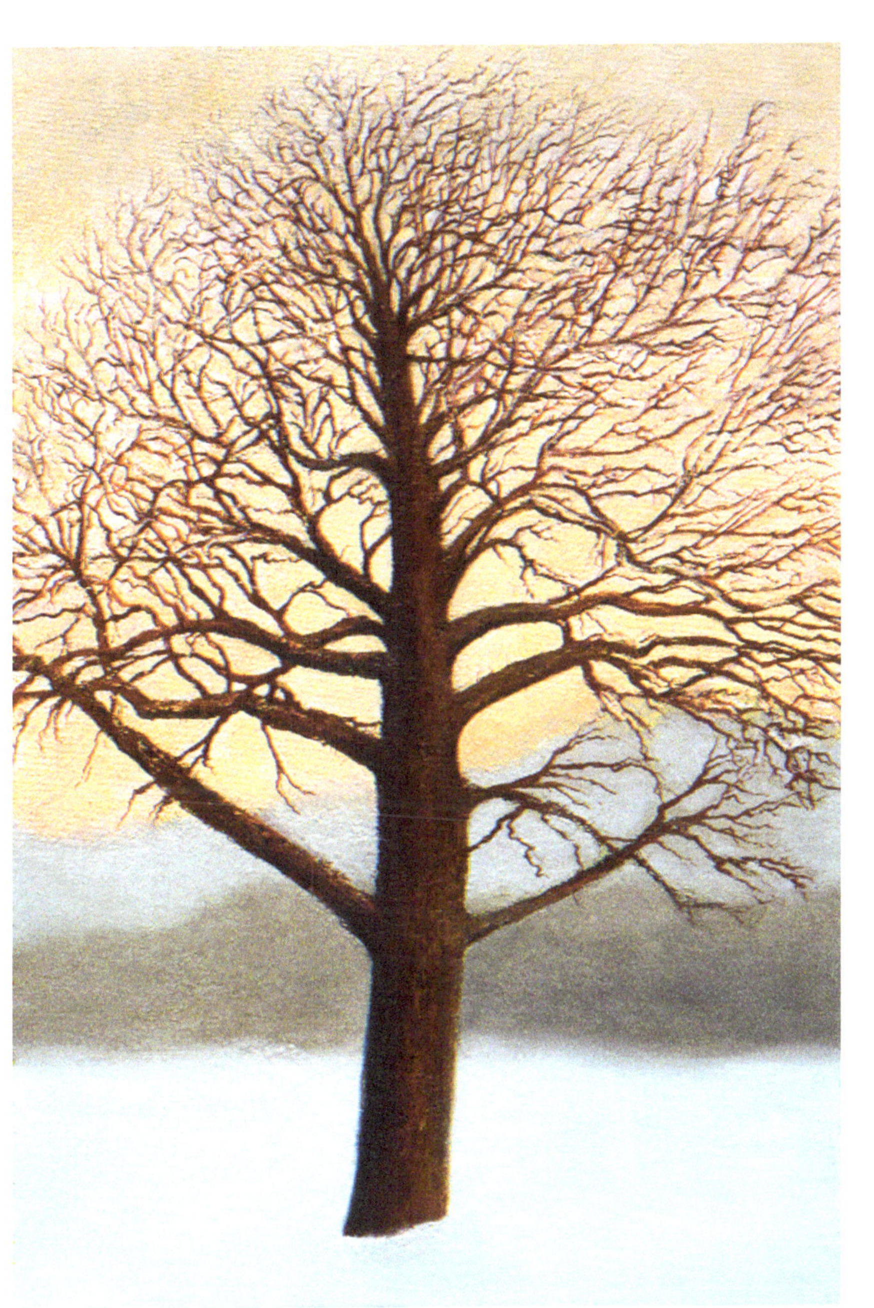

by the dairymen but welcomed by the bacteria that cause hoof infections. Unlike the barn, the parlor is well lit. Fluorescent light glints from the stainless steel tanks that temporarily store the fresh milk. (It is not generally known that each cow must consume a pound of milk chocolate, every day, in order to produce chocolate milk).

Afterwards, the herd saunters outside to loiter and stomp in the frigid darkness. The Hour of the Cow has arrived—forget the wolf—an interval of profound stillness in which the passage of time seems to have all but ceased.

February imposes long stretches in which the cows have nothing to do except listen to a drizzle of stringed instruments on the radio playing the music of Vivaldi.

Bovine psyhologists insist classical music calms the herd, though some cows yearn for heavy metal rock with the volume cranked.

Daydreaming provides welcome diversion: Some cows long to wander through verdant sunlit fields, bellowing ancient bovine monody (having yet to master polyphony).

Others yearn to board a cruise ship and devote each indolent day to shuffleboard, eating canapés and swallowing beverages equipped with swizzle sticks shaped like tiny umbrellas. For the dairymen paradise consists of a Lazy-Boy recliner, cheeseburgers, an ample supply of beer and a Patriots game on television.

A streak of charcoal grey begins to brighten the eastern horizon, signaling the end of another long winter night. The cows huddle quietly in the gloom and look to the sky in hopes of catching a glimpse of their favorite constellation, which is, of course, Taurus, the bull. Each cow emits carbon dioxide at one end and methane at the other, unaware of the latter's dire potency as a greenhouse gas. Steam rises from each broad back before dissipating in the silent blue eternity of a February morning.

March

AS IN ALL TRANSITIONS from one month to the next, the early days of March are indistinguishable from those at the close of February. Zero degree mornings are still common but by the end of the month old man winter has lost his grip. The cows spend less time in the barn each day. Instead, they traipse through colorless fields in search of something green, a hue banished by winter's monochromatic tyranny.

The sun continues its slow progress towards the zenith. An increase in the daily average temperature coincides with additional daylight, a welcome change for the herd, the herdsmen and the starlings that now perch on overhead wires. Although too soon for redwing blackbirds, the crows have returned after spending the winter in pool parlors in Newark and Philadelphia. Gliding overhead on lustrous black plumage, they congregate atop the tallest trees and cackle like deranged pterodactyls.

Cows are the dominant species in the barn but share it with feral cats. Lean, wiry and always hungry, barn cats are tolerated because they help keep the rodent population in check. Wary of humans, barn cats never see the inside of the farmhouse and are prone to making a mistake that costs them dearly. For often, in winter, a barn cat will sleep nestled against the warm flank of a drowsing cow. All is well until the cow rolls over during the night, squashing the cat and squelching whatever remained of its original nine lives. The mice cheer whenever one of their merciless foes is thus flattened.

Icicles hang from the barn's eaves. Droplets fall from their dagger-like tips as the strengthening noonday sun starts to melt a winter's accumulation of snow and ice. By mid afternoon the temperature has fallen, the drip-rate decreases and ceases entirely as the icy lock snicks shut until the following day.

By mid-month patches of bare ground appear in sheltered, south-facing nooks. The color green also reappears as the melting snow exposes a carpet of moss atop boulders. Trickles of melt water become rivulets, which swell as they meander towards Lake Champlain, several hundred yards to the west.

Most trees are not yet fully awake, although the hills now exhibit a subtle red blush as tiny new buds begin to swell. Sugaring season has begun. Farmers boil the maple sap that trickled through blue plastic tubing from tree to sugarhouse, a process made infinitely easier for men and the horses that pulled heavy, sap-laden sledges through the woods. The ubiquitous metal buckets that once hung from every maple trunk now hang in antique shops.

The vernal equinox occurs on March 21st. The sun's position at sunset is now at the midway point in its annual oscillation from south to north. Higher still, the constellation Leo occupies the zenith, the herd's least favorite.

By the end of the month honeybees shake off months of torpor by hovering around the entrance to a hive built within a hollow chiseled by a pileated woodpecker. Crocus tips poke through recently revealed soil. A late season snowfall could bury them but they long ago evolved the ability to withstand such an indignity. The snow will soon melt and a clutch of purple and yellow flowers will provide a miraculous sight after a long hard winter . . . undeniable evidence that spring has indeed sprung.

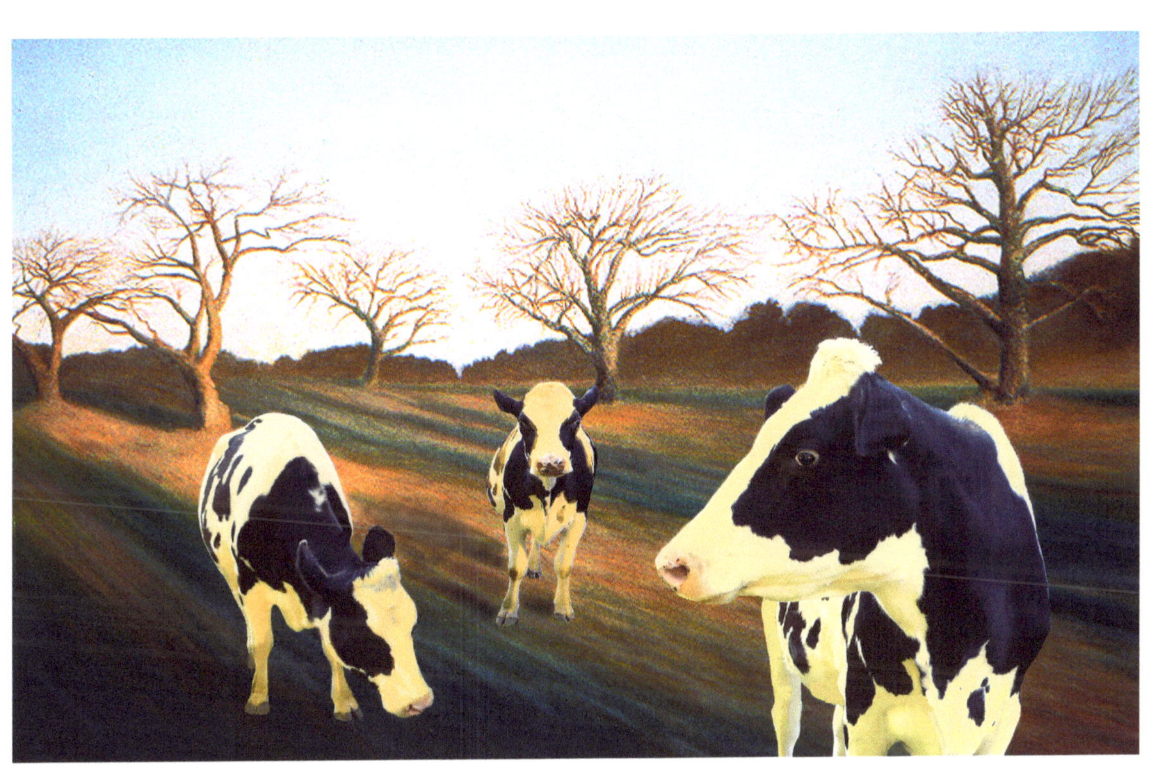

April

ASNOWSTORM IN APRIL is a possibility welcomed by skiers intent upon prolonging a rapturous flirtation with the force of gravity. The burgeoning heat of the sun quickly melts snow at lower elevations; runoff swells streams and floods low-lying fields but it will be many weeks before the seventy-inches atop mountain peaks is gone.

A watering hole used by the herd is still ice-capped. The surface reveals the pale green tint of algae, an indication of renewed cellular activity and the first sign of spring. The ice will soon melt, the pond's reopening announced by peepers whose ardor is undiminished by immersion in cold wet mud. Soon, the oasis will harbor thousands of tiny eggs within a milky scum, each housing a wriggling nodule. The majority of tadpoles are destined to provide food for insects, fish, birds and each other but enough always survive, thus assuring the continued existence of the summer frog choir.

A dry start to the month impedes the general greening of spring but eventual showers motivate buds to swell. Where previously the cows were able to see hundreds of yards into the surrounding woods, the profusion of expanding leaves form a fine green haze that obscures the view. Soon a green wall will completely shroud the forest.

The woods are no longer silent. A snare drum tattoo punctuates the air as woodpeckers chisel into pulpy dead wood for grubs. After careful experimentation, one enterprising woodpecker determined the exact spot on the

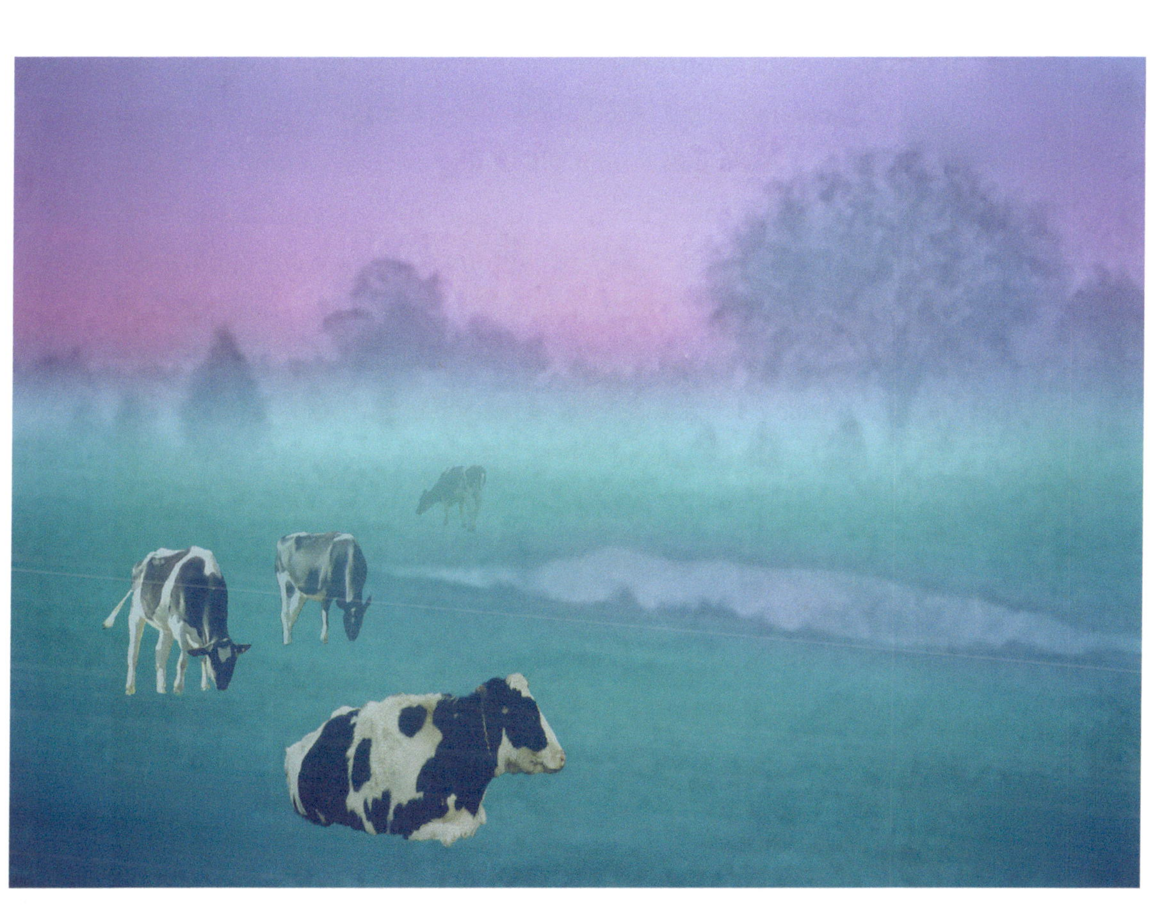

barn's outer wall where its hammering produced the loudest and therefore most impressive report.

April brings a fifth season—Mud Season—a time when back-country dirt roads deteriorate into a quagmire capable of swallowing a Volvo, ski-rack and all. April showers do indeed bring May flowers but not until after a prolonged inundation creates even more mud. The cows have been stomping through the muck for weeks and are now besmirched from hoof to haunch. Clods of caked mud adhere to every hide. The herd no longer bears any resemblance to the pristine black and white icons that adorn the trucks that transport a certain brand of ice cream to market. Although unfazed by each other's bedraggled appearance, one cow longs to immerse in a steaming bubblebath.

On mild afternoons the cows plod across the soggy meadow in search of edible shoots. The recently thawed ground reveals the brown matted residue from last year's vegetation. Ferns, however, always survive to provide a welcome splash of green.

Heifers become rambunctious in April and kick up their hind legs in a maneuver known as pronking in those parts of the world where antelope and gazelle run free. Curious and often bored, heifers sometimes behave like sullen teenagers who have just had their skateboards confiscated.

May

AFTER A MONTH dominated by clouds, mist and rain May provides glorious relief for herd and herdsmen alike. Sunlight dapples the ground. Leaves on every branch grow larger to form a dense canopy that creates shade for a drowsing herd. Dandelions now adorn the farmhouse lawn with a bright yellow carpet. Lilac blossoms perfume the air to provide synthesthesia between the color purple and a heavenly fragrance. Tulips, roses and shrubs contribute to the air already perfumed. A gentle zephry produces a soothing sussuration as it caresses every leaf.

The cows abandon the gloomy confines of the barn in favor of the open air. Whereas heifers were rambunctious in April, they go bonkers in May and gallop off at the slightest provocation, pausing to nibble succulent green shoots, convinced there is no such thing as a weed, only plants they have not yet been introduced to.

Black fly larvae emerge as adults from brooks to flit and bite. Mosquitoes rise up from stagnant water and take to the air in search of warm blood. An equally ravenous insect armada emerges in unimaginable numbers to crawl, hop, fly and torment. Ticks survived the winter hidden beneath the leaf litter but have become abundant as a result of climate change. It is no longer safe for a person to stretch out in a field for an idylic nap. The only beneficiaries are possums, which consider ticks a delicacy. Swallows swoop and dine on the bounteous bug buffet by day, leaving night to bats that dart and snatch with tactical sonar set to full-auto.

Migratory birds return in May to mate, build nests and lay eggs. Once the eggs hatch the parents stuff bug after bug into the gaping maw of each insatiable offspring. Soon fluffy chicks will exceed the size of their parents, but it will be weeks yet before the fledglings attend their first day of flight school. Ravens produce young and they, too, take to the air after sufficient instruction. Awkward and hesitant at first, the young master the art of flight but require much additional practice before their rude squawks bear any resemblance to the confidant caws emitted by their parents.

If a cow stayed up till two in the morning the constellation Cygnus would be seen rising in the east, a welcome sight for all who have had enough of Orion's winter dominance in the night sky.

The first thunderstorm of the season rumbles in from the west. Pitchforks of electricity skewer the air, split molecules and create a vacuum quickly filled in a process that produces thunder, the sound of angels bowling on a county-wide alley. At times, the sun breaks through while rain still falls to create an arc of radiant prismatic color.

And then it happens…

A cow is struck by a rainbow!

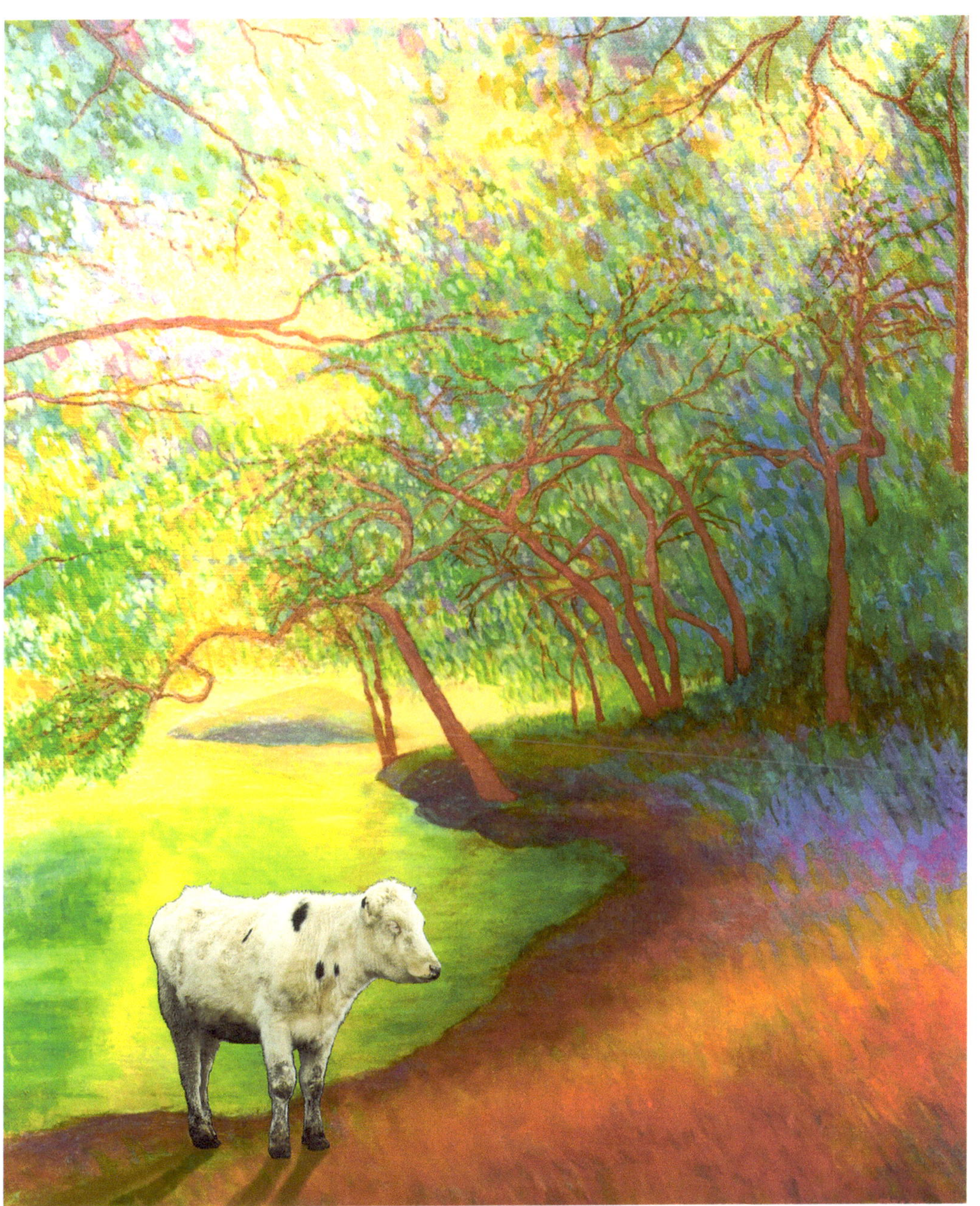

June

THE PROMISE OF RENEWAL made in May is fulfilled in June. Every plant riots quietly in the sun and the most recalcitrant old oak unfurls shiny new leaves. Conifers bloom and release clouds of saffron-colored pollen, particles that waft for miles before settling on the surface of ponds to form intricate yellow filigrees.

The herd savors the chlorophyll-laden air and even the most hide-bound bovine prances like a frisky calf. June's weather can be cool and wet or hot and dry. Either way, the cows long for the sultry days of summer as eagerly as a baseball fan awaiting the president's first pitch on opening day. (Jersey cows are Yankee fans, by the way, while Holsteins prefer the Red Sox). Regardless of allegiance, the herd is never quite convinced summer is here until they hear the boom of fireworks on the Fourth of July.

Although the tentative rumble of distant thunder was heard the previous month the season's first full-scale thunderstorm fires up in June. Purple strobo-scopic flashes, ground-shaking thunder and torrential rain inundate the cows as they huddle beneath a grove of maples, unaware of peril shared with golfers that sought shelter beneath a tree. The herd experienced a surge of patrio-tism the day Air Force One cruised majestically above the spine of the Green Mountains on its way to deliver the president to a campaign event in Burlington, Vermont's largest city. That night the cows caught a glimpse of the International Space Station as it orbited high above. Far brighter than any satellite, the bril-liant white dot silently traversed the sky at eighteen thousand miles an hour.

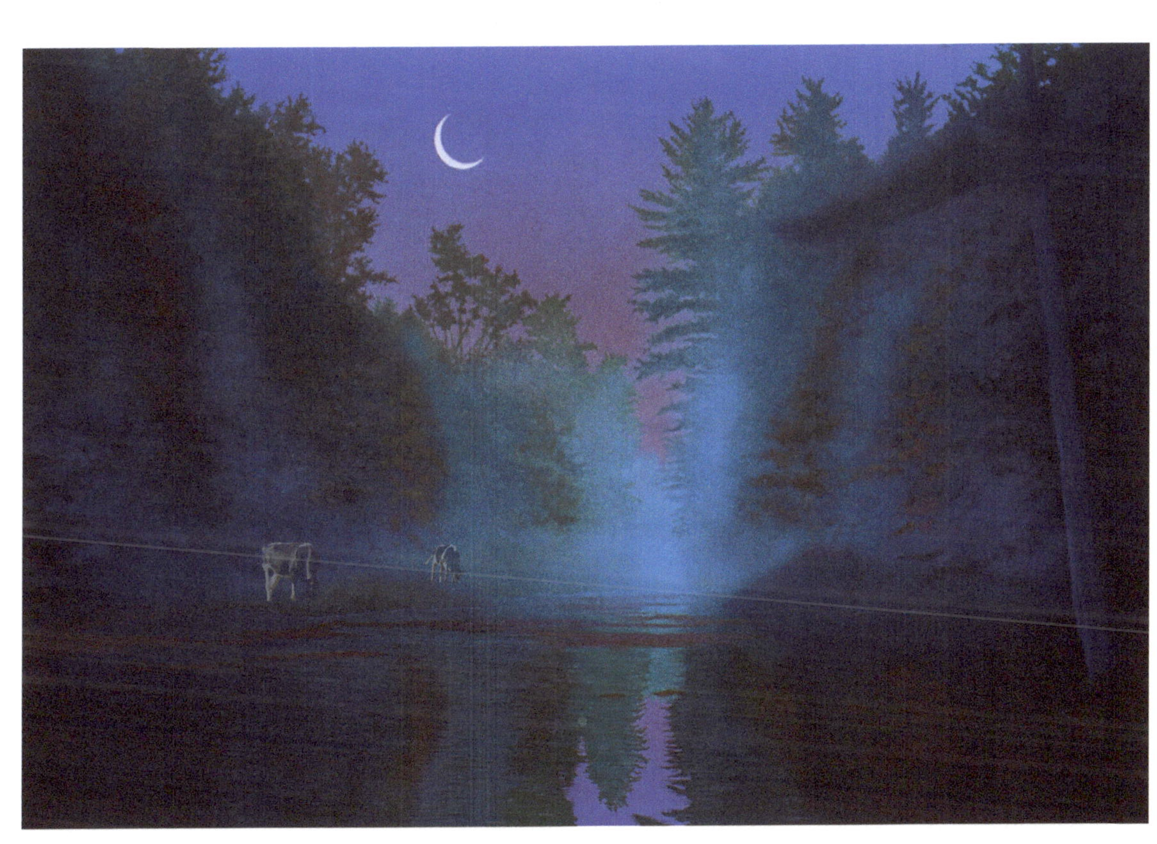

Late the following afternoon an observant cow happened to be looking in just the right place at just the right time to spot the space station in broad daylight. The sun had dipped behind the Green Mountains but not below the horizon and this allowed the space station's massive solar panels to reflect a brief but dazzling orange flash.

At night the Big Dipper appears to sit in an upright position, presumably to be refilled, as compared to other times of the year when it tilts to pour forth its contents. This celestial ladle has long been thought to convey water, but all cows know it was designed to dispense milk.

On June 21st, the Summer Solstice marks the longest day of the year. The sun sets at 8:40 p.m. Darkness does not prevail until eleven. Every ten years the full moon rises on this special evening and the cows conduct a solemn ceremony rarely, if ever, observed by their keepers. As evening draws nigh half the herd turns to face the moon's pale disk as it rises in the east while the other half turns toward the setting sun. At the precise moment both celestial spheres appear to hover just above their respective horizons, the lunar cows and the solar cows emit a long, soulful moo… an expression of bovine exaltation.

July

THE COWS AGREE: There is nothing in Vermont as fine or rare as a day in July. Shielded by June on one side and August on the other, the hottest days of the year loom. Heat and humidity banish all memory of the previous winter and all thought of the one to come. Sunflakes have been accumulating in drifts. Deflected for the most part by the Earth's magnetic field, the solar wind's torrent of charged particles breach this defense from time to time to ignite the Aurora, also known as the northern lights. Such a display often begins with a glow easily mistaken for the last light of day reflected by clouds.

It is said sitting cows foretell the approach of rain. Maybe so, but they understand the law of thermal dynamics and seek shade in which to drowse away an indolent afternoon, twitching their ears while peering into the blue haze that swallows the peaks of the Adirondack mountains on the western side of Lake Champlain. On such a hot day the cows limit exertion to rubbing against a tree trunk to scratch a hard to reach spot.

Unlike the dairymen, cows never complain about humidity. July evenings are filled with interesting sounds: The bellowing of a lovesick bull carries a long way in the moist still air. Separated by many acres and two stout fences, the cows sigh, bat their eyelashes and swoon with thoughts of forbidden passion. A pair of amorous pileated woodpeckers make tremulous whooping sounds as they chase one another at high speed, swerving around tree trunks. A skunk applies a dab of cologne behind each ear prior to venturing forth in search of true love. Foxes bark and gambol in the purple twilight, while glow-worms blush discreetly in the grass. Fireflies inspired by flashes of heat-lightning become aroused, take flight and transmit prurient suggestions to one another in a code far older than Morse's.

Now is a good time to clarify one of the great mysteries surrounding cows.... What is this so-called "cud" they've all been chewing?

As ruminant vegetarians, cows are equipped with not one but two stomachs. The first holds the recently swallowed grass, hay and Barn Mix granola but the extraction of nutrients from such a diet is time-consuming. And so, they transfer the cellulose-rich material from stomach to the mouth to undergo another round of chewing. The pulverized material then enters the second stomach for additional processing prior to an inevitable reunion with daylight.

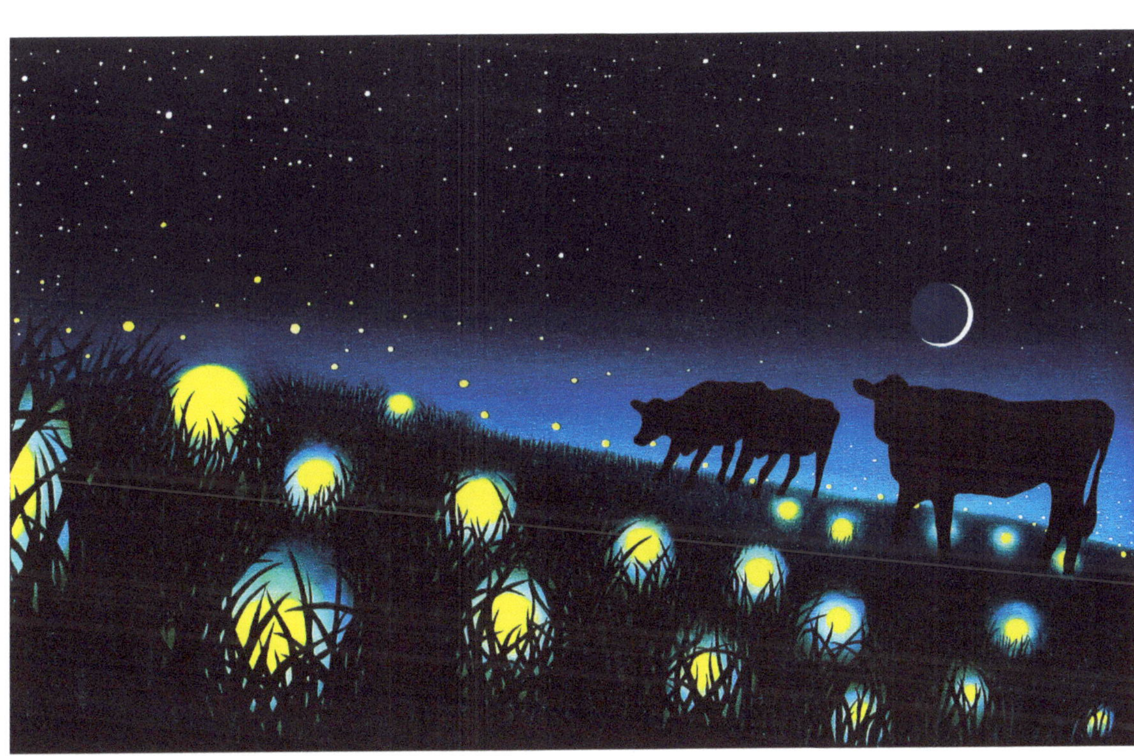

August

L IFE FOR THE HERD and herdsmen achieves unrivaled sweetness in August. The days are warm, the nights agreeably cool and the aroma of mown grass is never more evocative than when warmed by the August sun. Chicory is in full bloom. Blue flowers adorn the margins of every meadow, blossoms that radiate ultra-violet wavelengths in the segment of the electro-magnetic spectrum of particular interest to honeybees. This year's crop of milkweed pods have already begun to swell. Edible plants are now at their most succulent and the cows know such perfection can't last.

The length of each day continues to shrink. The sun's crimson orb now sets well before eight. Robins sing a timeless evening song as the empyrean afterglow lingers in the western sky. Chickadees nestle into feather beds. A cardinal's last flight of the day looks like a grey streak. As evening progresses huge rafts of geese gather to float and honk in the middle of Lake Champlain for a night of raucous carousing.

The August night sky is at its most active. Every year on the 12th the Earth's orbit passes through a debris cloud left long ago by a comet. Friction between the particles and the atmosphere produces the brightest shooting stars of the year. Some are large enough to produce an incandescent trail that takes a split second to fade. Known as the radiant, each of these meteors appears to emanate from the constellation Perseus, thereby giving the Perseid's their name. In years when the moon is full (or close to it) on the 12th its reflected brilliance washes out all

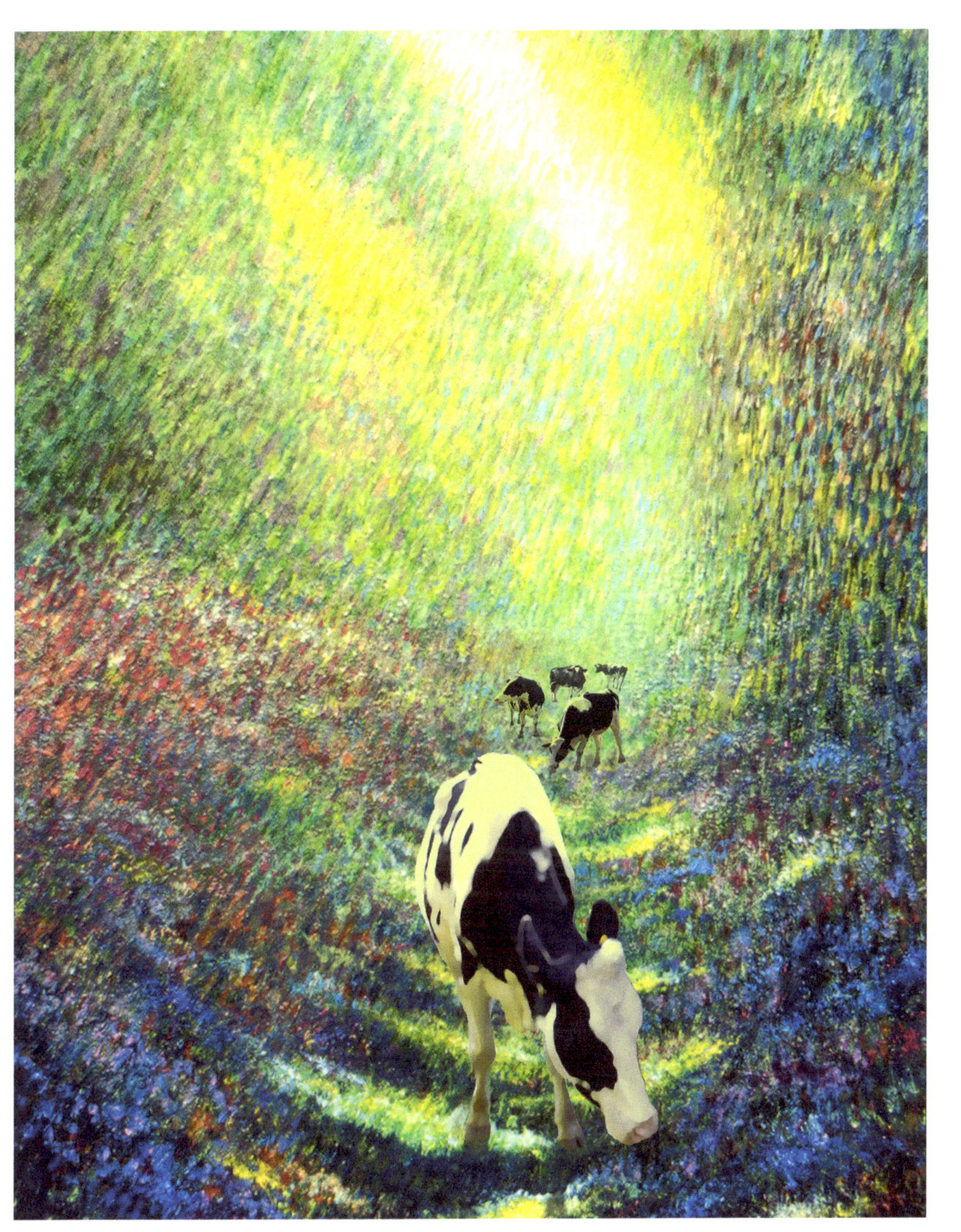

but the brightest meteors. When the moon is absent the depthless black abyss reveals cosmic spitballs that zip across all quadrants of the sky, especially after midnight. An elder member of the herd recalls seeing an exceptional display the night Perseid meteors streaked this way and that as the aurora produced shimmering curtains of saturated purple, blue, red and green.

During the latter half of the month cool evening air conveys the hint of fall. Apple trees are laden with fruit. Unpicked orbs eventually fall to the ground to feed deer, raccoons, chipmunks, birds and yellow-jackets. In August Mother Nature displays her most benign albeit capricious face. All wild creatures in Vermont are aware that the latter half of the feast or famine equation lurks not far in the future.

September Again

THE EARTH HAS COMPLETED another orbit around the Sun. It has been a peaceful year for herd and herdsmen alike. All well and good, you say, but *what* is the truth about cows? Ogden Nash wrote, "The cow is of the bovine ilk, one end moo the other milk."

True, but he omitted a quintessential detail . . . manure! A bovine byproduct produced as reliably as moo or milk, who can say which accumulates in the greatest amount? One thing is certain, dairymen deal with all three on a daily basis.

Once the grass, hay and granola reach the end of their journey through a cow's digestive system, the beast assumes a stance in which it bows all four legs. After lifting its tail the cow emits a steaming gush of manure. The slurry plops onto the ground and dries to form a cow-pie, a solid disk that can be picked up and flung like an organic Frisbee. Slurry is defined as "a suspension of a solid in a liquid," but conveys as much about manure as does the term "colloidal" in regard to ground coffee beans suspended in hot water. Slurry is brown paste that assaults the nose and sullies the ground.

Inside the barn on a daily basis the used cow food must be plowed into a threesided concrete bunker known as a lagoon. There, beneath plastic tarps held down by the weight of dozens of bald tires, it grows from mound to mountain. But what is to be done with this odiferous cache, you ask? The only option is to spread it across an open field, besmirching the ground like so much Bovril smeared on a piece of toast. Bovril, coincidentally, is mucilaginous brown goo made from beef byproducts (hooves!), a condiment consumed by certain fearless individuals in the British Isles.

The task of distributing such an enormous quantity of liquid waste begins when a tractor tows a spreader back and forth across a field of unsuspecting alfalfa. The spreader is nothing more than a wheeled metal tank equipped with a rotating nozzle atop the back end. When in operation a viscid plume sprays into the air, a geyser that hits the ground with a splat, a technique remarkably similar to the manner in which each cow divests itself of the same substance. Rainfall results in agricultural runoff, a problematic soup that fertilizes dangerous blue/green algae in Lake Champlain. The aromatic potency of freshly spread manure is strong and pervasive. Pungency begins to fade after a week or so, but the herdsman will continue to emit a faint molecular aroma for the rest of his days, regardless of how many hot soapy showers taken.

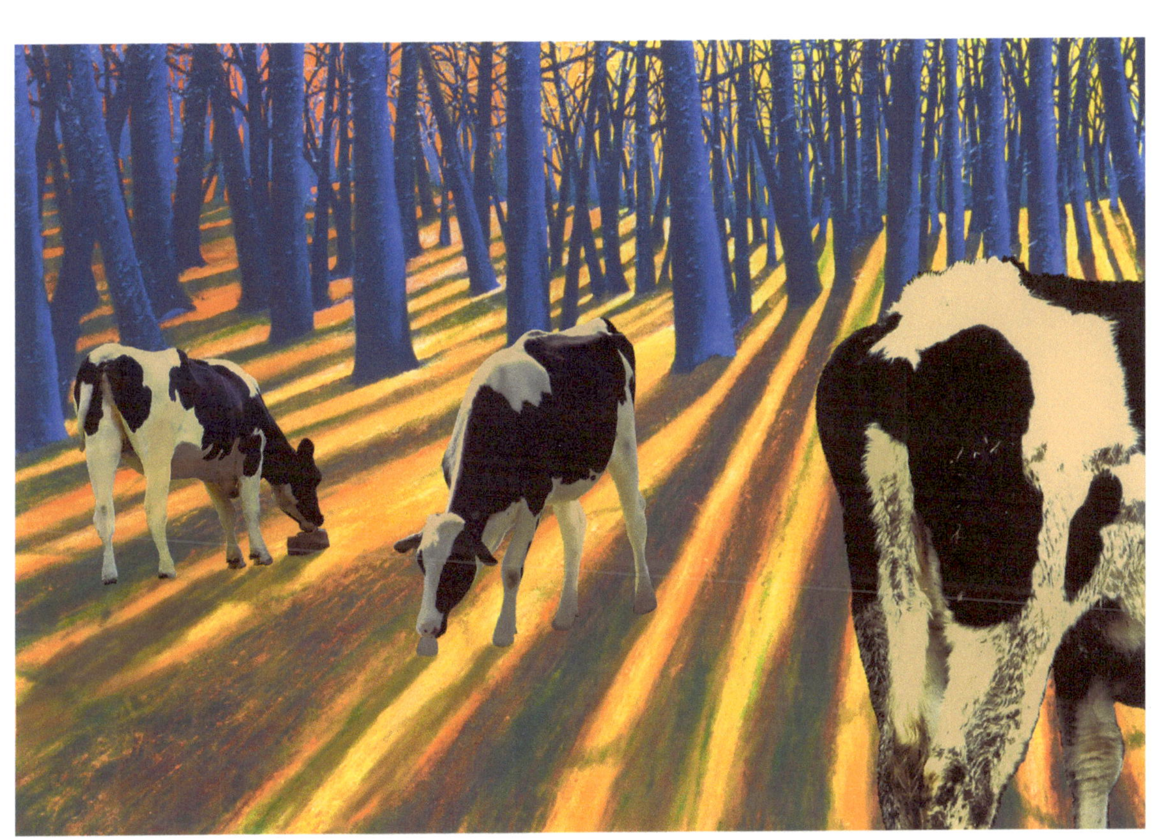

Epilogue

IN THE COURSE OF A YEAR the cows enjoyed many peaceful days and nights. They observed the rising and setting of the sun, the phases of the moon, the wandering of the planets and the swift silent passage of satellites—celestial sights denied to all who undergo television-induced catatonia until bedtime.

But *who*, you ask, is Hubble? And why is the pasture named after him?

Until relatively recently humanity peered into the night sky and confidently assumed that the five thousand or so stars visible to the naked eye comprised the entire cosmos. But in 1936 Edwin Hubble proved that our galaxy, the Milky Way, is but one among billions, unquestionably the most significant scientific discovery of the 20th century. Mr. Hubble also discovered that galaxies are not only expanding away from each other at a considerable gallop, but that the farther away they are the faster the recession. Astronomers have subsequently discovered that these galaxies are in fact accelerating!

No one knows why.

Our nearest galactic neighbor, the Andromeda galaxy is the only one visible to the naked eye. It is on a collision course with the Milky Way. Not to worry, though, for it will take an unimaginable amount of time before the two intersect. Even then, with such vast distances between individual stars, few will actually crash into one another.

Recently, the number of exoplanets detected orbiting stars other than our own has increased from a few to thousands. As this number continues to increase

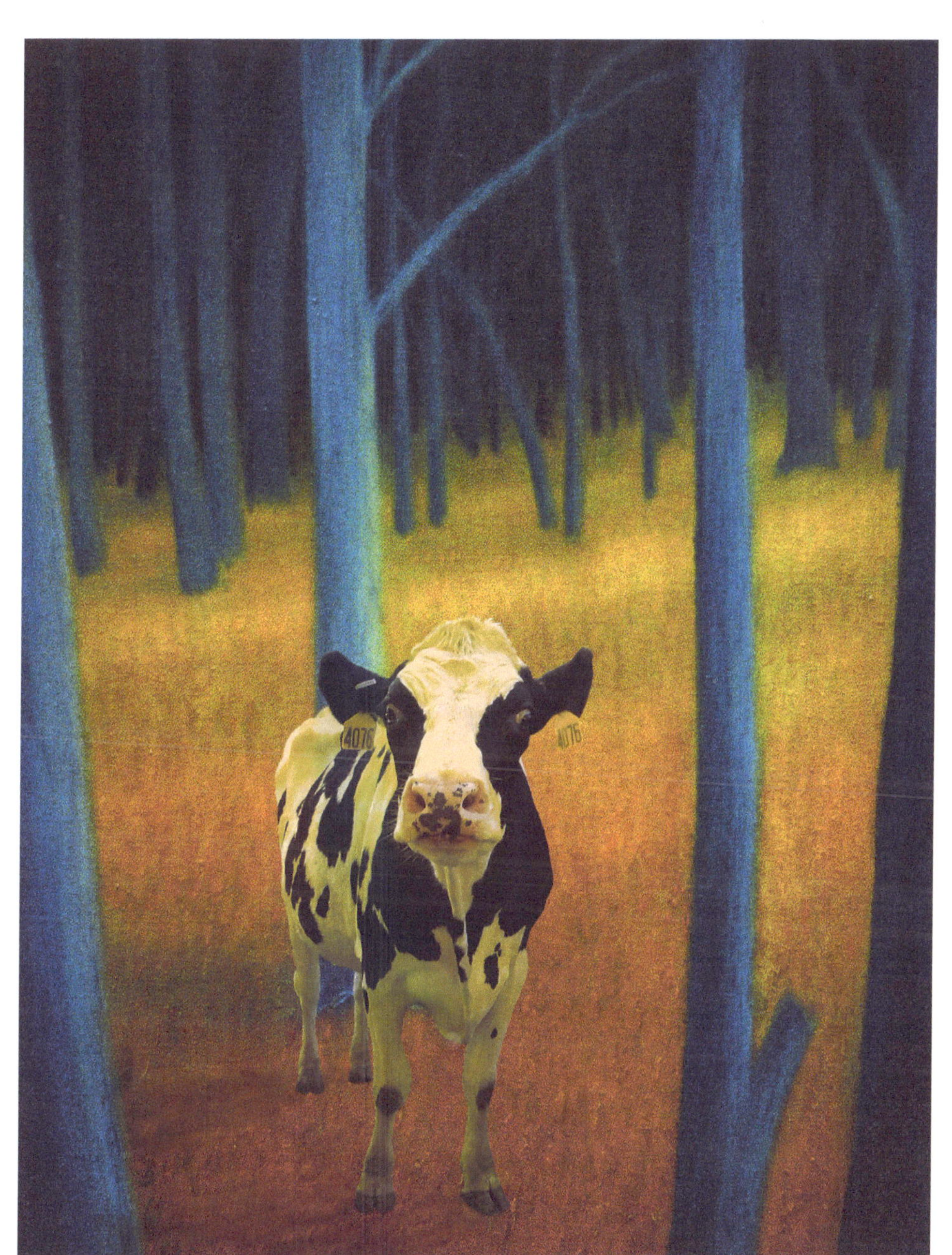

4076
4076

so, too, does the likelihood that life beyond the Earth abounds. One might then reasonably conclude that somewhere out there in the yawning chasm of space exist creatures best described as cows. Yet in spite of these astonishing developments many bovine mysteries here on Earth remain. Photographs taken by satellite revealed a hitherto unknown behavior in cows. When a herd anywhere in the world ambles into a field, why do they tend to orient themselves in positions that follow magnetic lines of orientation? Again, no one knows.

Be that as it may, here in Hubble's pasture the herd peers into the night sky and wonders who came up with the name Milky Way? An apt term, to be sure, but why was the Big Bang chosen to represent the creation of the universe instead of the Big Splash?

Although the origins of the universe are of no interest to the vast majority of our hooved friends, there's always one cowsmologist in every herd that grapples with the really Big Questions....

"Where did I come from?"

"How did the pasture come to be?"

"What is my place in the universe?"

And finally, the most intriguing question of all...

"Where does all the milk go?"

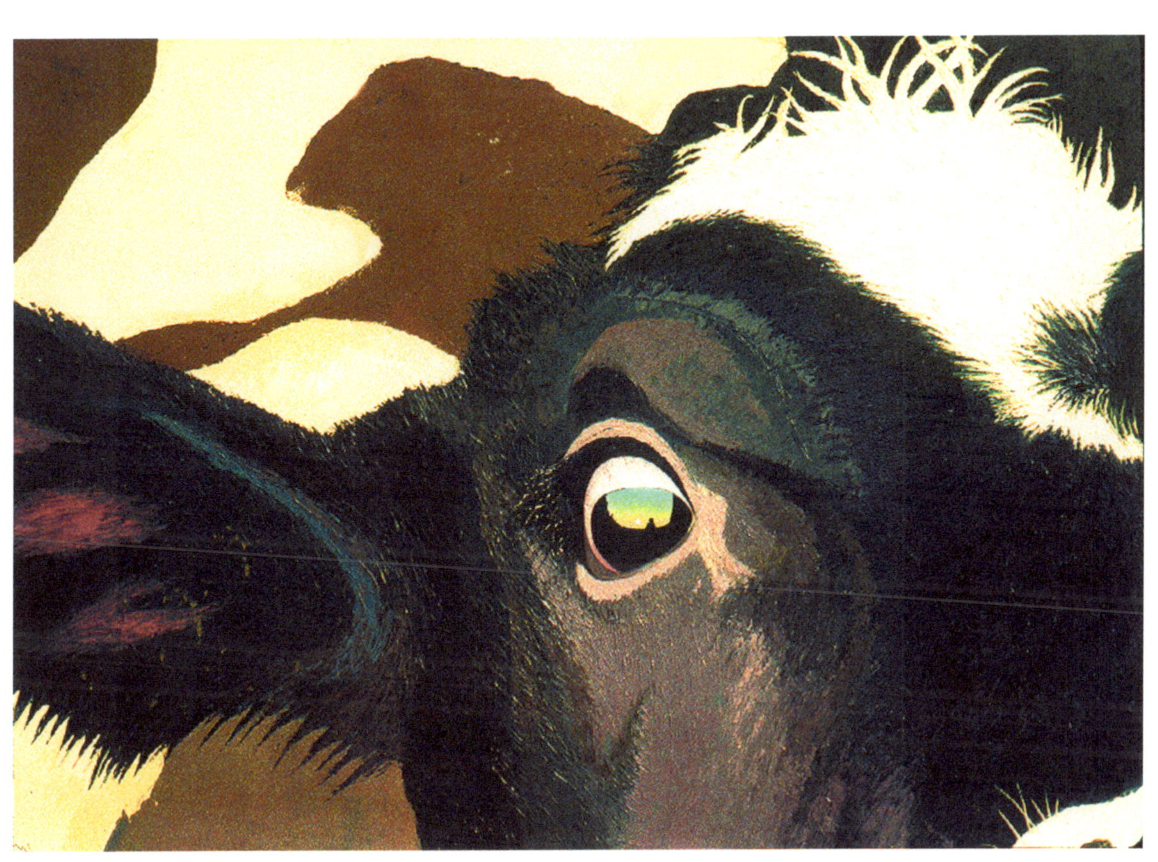

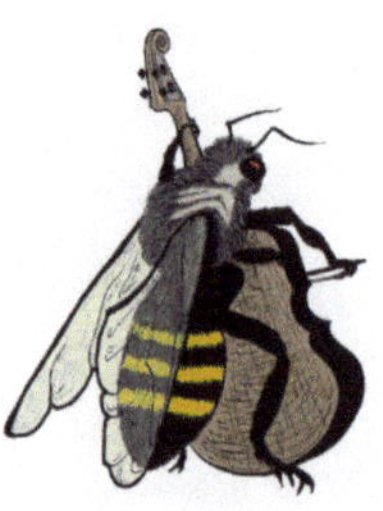

www.peterkieronwilliams.com

www.ingramcontent.com/pod-product-compliance
Lightning Source LLC
Chambersburg PA
CBHW042154030726
47599CB00004B/724